THE

MAKING OF A

MURDERER?

The REAL Steven Avery Story

Roger Harrington

Table of Contents

Introduction

The man known for Making A Murderer, the documentary of the darkest chapters of his life, was born by the name of Steven Avery on July 9th in 1962. A native of Manitowoc County in Wisconsin, the infamous events that birthed the television show series about him started with a wrongful conviction in 1985 for sexual assault and attempted murder. He was imprisoned for long enough to serve eighteen of the thirty-two years of his sentence before DNA evidence exonerated him and he was released. Two years later, the nightmare began anew when he faced a much longer sentence after being charged with murder.

After being exonerated in 2003, discussions were started about the criminal justice system in Wisconsin, which led to the Criminal Justice Reform Bill in 2005. This bill brought reforms into action that were meant to stop wrongful convictions in the future.

Also in 2003, Steven Avery filed a civil lawsuit for a total of $36 million that was aimed at Manitowoc County, its former district attorney, and its former sheriff and for his wrongful conviction and imprisonment. This civil suit for his previous wrongful conviction and imprisonment was still pending when he was arrested again in November of 2005. By 2007, he'd been convicted of the murder of a local photographer and was sentenced to life in prison with no possibility in the future for parole. Higher courts upheld this conviction, but in January of 2016, there was a new series of appeals.

In 2015, Netflix picked up the story of his 2007 murder trial for its original documentary series by the title of Making A Murderer. This documentary also touched on how his young nephew, Brendan Dassey, was pulled into the murder charges and arrested and convicted in 2007. Brendan Dassey was released in August of 2016 after a federal judge overturned his conviction based on evidence that his confession had not been made voluntarily.

The Early Life of Steven Avery

Steven Avery was born on July 9th in1962 to mother Dolores and father Allan Avery in Manitowoc County, Wisconsin. He has three siblings Chuck, Earl, and a sister by the name Barbara. In their early life, they lived on and worked on a 40-acre salvage yard in 1965 that was located on their property. Steven Avery was a student at schools that were focused on "slower kids" and located between Manitowoc and Mishicot. According to one of his lawyers, Steven Avery was tested there and the results said that his official IQ on his school records was only seventy. It was also said that while attending these schools throughout his childhood, that he "barely functioned in school."

Manitowoc County is a small town with two "different kinds of people" living within its limits; the upper/upper class and the working class. As a working class family, the Averys were already looked down upon by the upper/upper class in the area. Based solely on their social status, many people in town saw them as dirty and isolated. They were also accused of not taking part in the community, seeming to be people who did not care to be accepted as part of the town's community. Within Manitowoc County, most people pretend to be upper/upper class, whether or not they actually are. The Averys were known for not caring and not pretending or putting on airs; they were fine with being working class, which made them easily disliked by their peers and the people in town.

He got married to a woman and single mother by the name of Lori Mathiesen on July 24th of 1982 and together they had a total of four children by the names Rachel, Jenny, and their two twins, Steven and William.

His criminal history began at the young age of eighteen in March of 1981 when he was convicted of burglary after robbing a local bar with the assistance of a friend. He served a total sentence of two months in the Manitowoc County Jail after being sentenced to two years after being given probation and being ordered by the court to pay the bar back in restitution.

Over a year later, in a later month of the year 1982, two men came forward and confessed that Steven Avery had suggested that they throw his cat in a bonfire. Running on the suggestion of the more dominant male, they decided to do as they were told and threw the cat in the fire. It was said that Avery then threw oil and gasoline into the bonfire and they stood there together and watched the animal burn to death. After being convicted of animal cruelty after committing this crime, Steven Avery was put in jail, where he stayed until August of 1983.

In regards to these first two incarcerations, he was later quoted saying, "I was young and stupid, and hanging out with the wrong people" in his defense. His excuse involved him being young, impressionable and wanting to be deemed as "cool" by his troubled, troublemaking peers.

However, the trouble only continued in January of 1985 with his first cousin, Sandra Morris. As the wife of a Manitowoc County police officer, she was able to pressure the police to pursue her claims further and more fervently than they would any other random accusation. She went to the police and filed a report against Steven Avery, accusing him of hitting her car with his own car, forcing her to pull over, and then violently pointing a gun at her head while trying to physically force her to get into his car.

She also said that on previous occasions, whenever she would drive past his house, he would expose himself to her and wave his genitals around. Steven Avery admitted that the accusations she made against him that he'd run her off of the road and then pulled out a gun were true, though he claimed the gun was not loaded and his defense was that she had been spreading false rumors about him and he wanted her to stop. The sentence was six years for a charge of endangering safety while evincing a depraved mind and the possession of a firearm. However, the trouble caused by this crime would follow him for the rest of his life. According to Steven Avery, this was the incident that caused the Manitowoc County vendetta against him.

Steven Avery's cousin had connections within the Manitowoc County police department, which allowed her to hold a certain amount of sway over the investigation, according to the Avery family.

It also meant that when the investigation, court proceedings, and sentencing had been carried out and completed, the feeling of animosity may have still been present within the police department.

However, the gossip-mongering mentality of the small town that he lived in explains why Steven Avery was so upset about his first cousin spreading rumors about him. Within Manitowoc County, once a rumor was shared, people were prone to spreading it without bothering to look into its legitimacy. All it would take was a few simple words and Steven Avery's reputation would fall beyond repair. Residents of Manitowoc County, both past and present, have stated that they do not see someone pulling out a gun over rumors as farfetched. Some even say that they would see it as justified due to the irreparable damage caused to his reputation.

The Beginning of the End: The First Wrongful Conviction

While Steven Avery's past was not innocent before this wrongful conviction by any means, the real trouble began in July of 1985 when he was arrested for the brutal sexual assault and attack of a jogger by the name of Penny Beernsten on a beach at Lake Michigan. Some people would say that the trouble began with the altercation between himself and his first cousin, but this was the first time that law enforcement could really sink their teeth into him.

Penny Beernsten was jogging along a beach at Lake Michigan when she was attacked and raped by a man she had never seen before. When she spoke with police, she gave them a physical description that allowed them to create a photo line up that featured the faces of nine different men. Penny Beernsten chose Steven Avery's photo, and he was arrested the day afterward. The victim identified him in both a photo lineup and then a physical lineup, as well as in court in front of a jury, but Steven Avery had an alibi that said he was forty miles away that was supported by sixteen eyewitnesses and a receipt from Green Bay with a time stamp on it for 5:13 pm on the day of the assault. Penny stated that her attach happened sometime around 3:50 pm. In order for Steven Avery to have committed this crime, he would have had to attack Penny at 3:50pm, stick around for about fifteen minutes to complete his assault, leave the scene where the woman was attacked, cross a full mile of empty space in order to get to the parking lot, drive home, put his family and their travel belongings into the car, and make a forty-five minute drive; all in just over an hour's worth of time. According to one of the forensic examiners that worked for the state, there was a shirt on Steven Avery's shirt that could have come from Penny Beernsten. After the trial was concluded, the jury left the court room in order to deliberate. They just a short span of four hours before returning with their verdict. They made their decision based almost completely on the eyewitness account from Penny Beernsten, finding him guilty on December 14th of 1985.

He was still charged, which led to his conviction that sent him to prison for a sentence of thirty-two years for rape and attempted murder. He filed appeals that were denied by the higher courts in both 1987 and 1996.

A call was made to the Manitowoc County Jail by a police detective in Brown County after an inmate admitted that years before, he had assaulted someone in Manitowoc County and he had essentially gotten away with it because there was another person in jail for the crime. The officer at the jail sent the call to the Manitowoc County detective bureau, where Sheriff Kocourek ignored the information. Deputies in the office with him remembered hearing him say that they already had the right guy, so there was no need to concern themselves with this new and possibly exonerating confession.

Despite the dismissal from law enforcement, Steven Avery continued to say that he was innocent of the assault against Beerntsen. He had served eighteen years of his sentence in 2002, with the first six being served concurrently with the charges filed against him for the convictions for endangerment and weapons. In the same year, DNA testing was used by the Wisconsin Innocence Project by court order, which would eventually lead to the exoneration of Steven Avery by proving that the perpetrator was a man by the name of Gregory Allen.

DNA testing had not yet been invented and made available during the original investigation and trial, so it couldn't be used before, but there had been a substantial amount of DNA evidence underneath Penny Beernsten's fingernails when she had been examined after the attack. According to these DNA tests, the DNA belonged to an unknown person. However, these tests were not able to immediately exonerate Steven Avery, because it could not be immediately proven that the DNA was not his. His motions for a new trial were denied.

Again, the Wisconsin Innocence Project worked to get another court order, this time for the testing of thirteen different hairs that had been recovered off of Penny Beernsten during the investigation after her sexual assault. After being taken to the state crime laboratory, the FBI database that stored DNA records finally pointed away from Steven Avery. The real perpetrator was a man by the name of Gregory Allen, and he happened to be a convicted felon that was already serving a sentence of sixty years for sexually assaulted another woman in the Green Bay area after he had momentarily gotten away with attacking Penny Beernsten.

Gregory Allen was said to look very similar to Steven Avery and Allen had a history of criminal behavior against women that included a previous assault in 1983 on the same beach, leading the police to put him under official surveillance in 1985, though photos of Gregory Allen were not present in the photo lineup and he was not present for the physical lineup either. He was not considered to be a suspect in the assault against Beerntsen until the DNA evidence proved him to be guilty, despite his history.

With a new suspect successfully proven guilty, there was nothing left but for the Manitowox District Attorney's Office to accept a request to dismiss all of the charges against Steven Avery. The man was released.

Freedom was finally given to Steven Avery on September 11th of 2003 with his official release, but his life was already in ruins. His happy family life was torn apart, with his family being estranged and his wife having divorced him while he was in prison. The court issued an order while he was incarcerated that kept him away from his children by limiting the amount of contact he was allowed to have with him. As evidence to bring the order to life, allegations of emotional and physical abuse towards both his wife and his children were cited. The conviction that put him in jail had already caught the widespread attention of everyone in town. His reputation was ruined, and regardless of the legal status of the charges that put him in jail, he was seen locally as guilty.

In response to Steven Avery's wrongful imprisonment, the Republican chairman of the Wisconsin Assembly Judiciary Committee created a bipartisan task force with the intention of recommending improvements that would affect the state's criminal justice system with the hope of lowering the amount of wrongful convictions and imprisonments in the future. Some of these recommendations were focused on changing the eyewitness identification protocol process for the better while others focused on making new guidelines for officers that are interrogating both suspects and witnesses. These new recommendations also covered and changed the guidelines for collecting and storing the material evidence involved in crimes. All of these recommendations were put together and drafted into legislation. This legislation was named the Avery Bill, and it was signed and passed in October of 2005. A month later, Steven Avery was charged with another crime and the legislation was rebranded under the new name the Criminal Justice Reform Bill.

After the first wrongful conviction and imprisonment, Steven Avery took legal ramifications against Manitowoc Count, its former district attorney (Denis Vogel), and its former sheriff (Thomas Kocourek) in the form of a civil lawsuit. The end goal of this civil lawsuit was to collect a total of $36 million that he believed he was due to make up for the damages that his wrongful conviction caused. In February of 2006, this civil lawsuit was settled and closed for $400,000 after he was indicted a second time, this time for murder.

Out of 174 total inmates nationwide, Steven Avery was the only inmate involved in the Innocence Project to face a charge for a violent crime as of May of 2006. If the actual culprit for the rape of Penny Beernsten had been arrested and convicted instead of being allowed to hide behind Steven Avery's wrongful conviction for the crime he had committed, the real perpetrator would have been set free after serving his full sentence in

2016 at the earliest. However, Gregory Allen managed to evade the law for almost twenty years, despite having confessed to his crime to another officer at another prison. His confession, and the statement given by the officer that took it, were both discarded when they were given. Nobody gave the theory that Steven Avery was innocent any time until after DNA evidence exonerated him beyond a shadow of reasonable doubt. This ignorance towards the truth, even as it was shoved under the noses of law enforcement, only adds to the theory that they had a vendetta against Steven Avery and were determined to put him behind bars for as close to forever as possible.

Ironically enough, Steven Avery and the real rapist of Penny Beernsten -a man by the name of Gregory Allen- almost met each other in prison.

Another Big Arrest: The Halbach Murder

On October 31st in 2005, a photographer by the name of Teresa Halbach went missing. After a period of time, her parents called police to report her missing on the 3rd of November in the same year. She was born in Kaukauna, Wisconsin on March 22nd in 1980. According to her appointment scheduler, the last person she had seen before disappearing was Steven Avery. She was to meet him at his house to take photos of a minivan that belonged to his sister and he was putting up for sale. An investigation into Teresa Halbach's disappearance brought the investigation to a salvage yard, where they found her car partially hidden. Inside the car, they found bloodstains. The DNA in these bloodstains was a match to Steven Avery. Later, the investigation uncovered charred bone fragments in a fire pit near Steven Avery's home, and these bone fragments were a match to Teresa Halbach.

After her Toyota RAV4 was found and investigated, the Calumet County Sheriff by the name of Jerry Pagel followed the evidence to the Halbach property on November 10th of 2005. During the investigation of the Avery Salvage Yard and the surrounding Avery property, charred remains of human origin were found in a fire pit. Her car key, her cell phone, and her license plates were also found on the Avery property. Further investigation of the evidence that had been found continued, and the DNA found in her car was tested and on November 15th, Avery was arrested as the number one suspect in the murder of Teresa Halbach. The blood inside of Teresa Halbach's abandoned vehicle belonged to Steven Avery, and the charges he faced were the possession of an illegal firearm, kidnapping, murder, and the mutilation of a dead body.

With all suspicious fingers pointing at Steven Avery, the man was arrested on November 11th of 2005 as the number one suspect and was charged with the murder of Teresa Halbach, on top of kidnapping, sexual assault, and the mutilation of a dead body. By this point, he was already a convicted felon and he'd already been charged after breaking the law through a weapons violation.

According to Steven Avery, the entire murder investigation was nothing more than a purposeful frame job that the police perpetrated in order to discredit him and ruin his pending lawsuit for his previous wrongful conviction. Because of this pending lawsuit, the Manitowoc County police department handed over the control of the murder investigation, putting Calumet County and their Sheriff's Department in charge. However, the sheriff's deputies from Manitowoc County were given tasks to complete for the case that included repeatedly searching the home of Steven Avery as well as his garage and the rest of his property. They were supervised by the officers from Calumet County, but it was a Manitowoc County deputy that was responsible for finding the key to Teresa

Halbach's car, hidden in Steven Avery's trailer in his bedroom. According to Steven Avery's attorneys, this inclusion of Manitowoc County officers in the investigation was a solid conflict of interest and accused them of possible tampering with evidence.

Steven Avery's alibi relied heavily on the testimony of his young nephew, Brendan Dassey. The sixteen year old boy was intensely interrogated without any form of legal representation present. His parents were not there either, and the police that were investigating the crime and interrogating Brendan Dassey fed him false information and made false promises to him. After some time, the boy broke down and gave a confession that gave him a part in both the rape and murder of Teresa Halbach, as well as giving him a part in the mutilation of her dead body. In later investigations, the confession given by Brendan was deemed clearly involuntary by the expert opinion of a U.S. magistrate judge.

While setting up Steven Avery's defense, his attorneys checked the old evidence against him that had been collected during the trails in 1996 Beerntsen case and found that inside one of the evidence boxes, a vial of Steven Avery's blood had been tampered with. There was a puncture hole in the lid, which put reasonable doubt on the blood evidence found in Teresa Halbach's vehicle. The defense team speculated that it was possible that the Manitowoc County police had drawn the blood from the evidence vial and had planted it in Teresa Halbach's car in order to incriminate Steven Avery. Reasons behind this possibility included retaliation for his civil lawsuit and a vendetta from earlier cases; it was suggested that the police department wanted to catch Steven Avery at all costs because they had failed to keep him behind bars any of the other times he had brushed shoulders with the law. However, the FBI did their own tests on the blood evidence that was found, and in that testing, they looked for traces of ethylenediaminetetraacetic acid, otherwise known as EDTA. The reason for this was simple; EDTA is used as a preservative for blood vials to make sure that the blood evidence stays fresh and EDTA is not found naturally within the human body. The lack of EDTA found in the blood samples from Teresa Halbach's vehicle pointed to the theory that the blood had come directly out of Steven Avery and not from a blood vial. His defense team brought witnesses to the stand that would then testify that being unable to find any trace of EDTA did not mean that there was none present, it just meant that the test was inconclusive.

The criminal charges for the Avery family doubled when Steven Avery's nephew, Brendan Dassey, was charged in March of 2006 as an accessory to the crimes against Teresa Halbach. He confessed under duress while being interrogated, saying that he had helped his uncle (Steven Avery) murder and then hide Teresa Halbach's body. Later, Brendan Dassey recanted, taking his confession back and claiming that the police had coerced him into making the original confession. He also refused to take part in his uncle's trial and would not speak against him. In his own trial, Brendan Dassey was convicted and found guilty of rape, murder, and the mutilation of a dead body.

During the pre-trial hearings that took place in January of 2007, sexual assault and kidnapping were both taken off of the list of charges. In March of the same year, Steven Avery faced the remaining charges when he made it to trial in Calumet County. The leader of the prosecution team was a District Attorney from Calumet by the name of Ken Kratz. The judge was a man from the Manitowoc County Circuit Court by the name of Judge Patrick Willis. The trial came to a close on March 18th, with Steven Avery being found guilty of illegal possession of a firearm and the much larger charge of first-degree murder. On the charge for mutilating a corpse, he was acquitted. Six weeks after the guilty verdict was reached, his sentence for the murder charge was announced and Steven Avery found himself facing life in prison without the possibility for parole. On top of that, he was given an additional five years behind bars for the illegal firearm charge. These two sentences were to be run concurrently, meaning he was able to serve them both at the same time instead of adding five years to the end of his life sentence.

The first five years of Steven Avery's sentence were spent in Boscobel at the Wisconsin Secure Program Facility, after which he was transferred to Waupun to stay in the Waupun Correctional Institution in 2012.

Making A Murderer was released on Netflix in January of 2016, inspiring People magazine to look into the case. They found out that one of the juror's wives worked with Manitowoc County as a clerk and another one of his jurors was father to one of the Sheriff's deputies in Manitowoc County. The addition of these two people from Manitowoc County in Steven Avery's trial defeated the purpose of hosting his trial outside of the county that was accused of having a vendetta against him.

One of the jurors, a man by the name of Richard Mahler, was excused from his duties for Steven Avery's trial after a family emergency pulled him away from deliberations, but he spoke about his time within the trial at a later date. According to him, there was an informal vote that took place before the trial even began and seven of the people on the jury lineup thought that he was not guilty. In fact, he was shocked and surprised that a guilty verdict was agreed upon. Some have disagreed with Richard Mahler's account, saying that there had been no early vote had taken place, but instead said that there was an informal vote that took place later that showed only three of the jurors thought he wasn't guilty. A third member of the jury team was alleged to have spoken with the filmmakers behind the documentary Making a Murderer came out. This juror claimed to have felt intimidated, as though there were a reason to fear for his own personal safety if he did not deliver a guilty verdict.

The state officially denied Steven Avery's petition to earn himself a new trial in August of 2001 through the state appeals court system. In 2013, a motion that had been filed in order to have the ruling reviewed was denied by the Wisconsin Supreme Court. The Midwest Innocence Project had to collaborate with a Chicago attorney by the name of Kathleen Zellner in order to file another new appeal. The citations for this new appeal featured claims that Steven Avery's right to due process was violated, and it also accused the police officials that had gathered evidence of searching for these pieces of evidence in places that were beyond the reach of the search warrant that they had.

On the other case attached to the disappearance and murder of Teresa Halbach was Brendan Dassey, who went through his defense attorneys in order to file a writ of habeas corpus, which was brought to federal district court in December of 2015.

This writ asked that Brendan Dassey either be released or given another trial, claiming that his constitutional rights had been violated when he had been coerced into confessing that he had participated in murdering Teresa Halbach and hiding her body as well as the ineffective assistance of his previous counsel. Federal Magistrate William E. Duffin was there to overturn his conviction in August of 2016. His ruling stated that the confession given had been involuntary, and was therefore inadmissible. The same federal Magistrate allowed the defense to petition for Brendan Dassey's release from his imprisonment on the 14th of November, but that decision was overturned by November 17th by an appeals court. This decision was an order that stated that Brendan Dassey was to remain behind bars until the state's appeal could reach a decision on his habeas corpus writ. Two years later in June of 2017, the Magistrate's decision was upheld by the Seventh Circuit. This left the state with a short list of options; dismiss the charges completely, appeal to the ruling left by William E. Duffin, or start the process all over again with an official retrial.

Kathleen Zellner was also responsible for filing a motion on August 26th or 2016 that asked that the evidence in the case be re-examined, though this scientific testing would be happening post-conviction. This motion was answered by Judge Angela Sutkiewicz, who signed the order and officially asked that the evidence be scientifically tested again, starting on November 23rd of 2016.

After that small victory, Kathleen Zellner continued to do everything that she could for her client by writing and filing a post-conviction motion that spanned 1,272 pages and cited violations of the Brady laws, told of an ineffective counsel that led to a lack of assistance, and multiple written affidavits that had been given by experts in the field that argued with what the defense said was Teresa Halbach's cause of death and the way that she died. Also included in this motion were ethical violations in the prosecution perpetrated by the DA in Calumet County, D.A. Ken Kratz and a bunch of new evidence that had been found since the original trial. According to Kathleen Zellner, the entirety of the case against Steven Avery rested on the backs of a bunch of evidence that was planted by the police as well as multiple pieces of false testimony. Because of the content within the 1,272 page motion, Kathleen Zellner asked that a new trial be given to Steven Avery for the sake of true justice.

A petition that was entitled "investigate and pardon the Averys in Wisconsin and punish the corrupt officials who railroaded these innocent men" was created online on the internet at petitions.Whitehouse.gov on December 20th of 2015. A response was later given in January 2016 by a White House speaker that said that the President couldn't pardon either the man known as Steven Avery or his young nephew, Brendan Dassey because they both were prisoners of the state. Only an appropriate authority that worked at the state level would be useful in giving these two men the pardon that they both desired. But according to a spokes person for the Wisconsin governor's office by the name of Scott Walker, there were no plans to consider pardoning Steven Avery for the crimes that he was accused of.

Even though a second petition was also submitted online on the internet to the website petition.Whitehouse.gov on January 7th of 2017 with the title "initiate a federal investigation of the sheriff's office of Manitowoc County and Camulet County in Wisconsin." But because it didn't have the minimum number of signatures required to put the petition into operation, the petition was archived instead of being passed.

Brendan Dassey's Part In The Halbach Case

Born Brendan Ray Dassey on October 19th in 1989, the man is most well-known for his part in the Halbach case. A resident of Manitowoc County in Wisconsin by birth, he is the young nephew of Steven Avery. His most well-known moments are also his darkest, and they all involve the murder of Teresa Halbach. At the young age of sixteen, he was interrogated, incarcerated, tried, and convicted of being party to first-degree murder, second-degree sexual assault, and the mutilation of a corpse. He was sentenced to the lengthy sentence of life in prison though he was given the possibility of parole in the year 2048.

Along with those dark times, Brendan Dassey had three brothers and a half-brother. His full brothers were Bobby, Blaine, and Bryan and his half-brother was Brad. His mother was Barbara Dassey and his father was Peter Dassey. They divorced, leaving Brendan and his brothers living with their mother. Their large family home was located on property that was associated with the Avery Salvage Yard. Other residents of this property included Steven Avery.

When he was arrested, Brendan Dassey was just a sophomore at Mishicot High School at the young age of sixteen. His IQ was low enough that it bordered the line of official deficiency, making him much slower than his peers and putting him in classes geared towards special education. According to the people that knew him before the disappearance and murder of Teresa Halbach said that he was an introverted boy with a quiet demeanor. He liked animals, Westlemania, and video games. The case against him that connected him to the murder of Teresa Halbach was his first brush with the law. He did not have any involvement in any kind of crime and he did not have any records within the criminal justice system and no prior arrests.

Despite his clean record, Brendan Dassey was arrested on March 3rd in 2006 and faced charges that included being an accessory to first-degree homicide murder, the mutilation of a dead body, and sexual assault based on his coerced confession. Ken Kratz was the special prosecutor on the case and he was quick to hold a major press conference so that he could give the public information about the charges against Steven Avery and Brendan Dassey. Parts of Brendan Dassey's confession were read out loud, verbatim, during this press conference, which was covered by both newspapers and television media.

After being arrested, he was interrogated and eventually gave a confession that stated that he had helped his uncle Steven Avery kill Teresa Halbach and then helped to hide her body in an attempt to cover up the crime. His interrogation was filmed and shown at the trial, and parts of it also ended up becoming part of the original documentary by Netflix about Steven Avery by the title of Making A Murderer. When asked about his recanted confession later, Brendan Dassey said that the ideas that were not fed to him by law enforcement had been taken out of a book.

These interrogations were spread out in four parts of a span of forty-eight hours. Three of these interrogations occurred within twenty-four hours and there was no parent of guardian present and he was not given legal counsel or representation. The first place he was interrogated was his own family cabin, located in Crivitz through the practice of the Reid technique.

The Reid technique is the name for a specific type of interrogation questioning that was created by a man by the name of John Reid. As a polygraph expert and a consultant, he created this technique in order to test the credibility of the suspects being questioned. It is said by those that support this method of interrogation that it can successfully extract information from suspects that are otherwise unwilling to help law enforcement with their investigations or may be holding information back. Those against this technique argue that it is more important to remember that this technique can be responsible for people giving false confessions; it is known especially for making innocent children confess to things that they did not do. This technique splits the interrogation process into three phases. The first phase analyses the facts. The second phase analyses the behavior of the suspect during the interview. The final phase is not always necessary, but it is called the Reid Nine Steps of Interrogation. The biggest factor in this interrogation process is that law enforcement is accusatory, that they tell the suspect that based on the evidence, there is no way that they are not guilty. This interrogation technique relies more on factual-sounding monologues that state positively that the suspect is guilty, instead of asking them if they are. While the interrogator will remain positive that the suspect is guilty and continue to press the idea that they already have enough evidence to have the suspect convicted, the interrogator's behavior and demeanor is meant to remain patient, understanding, and they are not to demean the suspect. In essence, the interrogator will pretend to be the suspect's friend, seemingly offering them a kinder and gentler way out of a clear-cut situation that could only go terribly for them if they decide to not cooperate. It works on the basis of trust, trying to make the suspect feel as though they can comfortably tell their interrogator the truth. The interrogator will even justify the crime(s) the suspect is being accused of, trying to become friendly with the suspect by claiming that they understand their motives and find the end result to be perfectly reasonable.

Not surprisingly, Brendan Dassey's confession was later recanted and he had to inform his defense counsel of his side of the interrogation story. He also claimed that those that were supposed to be on his side were instead collaborating with the prosecution in order to get him to plead guilty. If he pled guilty, then the prosecution could call him as a witness and make him testify against his uncle, Steven Avery. Brendan Dassey continuously refused to testify against his uncle. Eventually, the people on his defense counsel were fired and replaced.

During his trial, the first lawyer that was assigned to his case was dismissed by the court itself on August 26th of 2006, because the lawyer had not been at Brendan's side during the interrogations he endured on May 13th. This was an absence of choice and was taken as a sign that he was not righteously determined to do his best. This first lawyer was then replaced by two different public defenders.

The trial of Brendan Dassey officially began on April 16th in 2007. The jury that gathered to judge his innocence against the charges against him were gathered from Dane County in Wisconsin, putting them outside of the controversial Manitowoc County citizens, and even the investigating Calumet County. The entirety of the trial spanned a total of nine days. The official verdict was given on April 25th of 2007. It took the jury a total of four hours to deliberate before deciding that Brendan Dassey was guilty. He was charged with first-degree intentional homicide, the mutilation of a dead body, as well as rape. At this point, he was only seventeen years old, but he was both tried and convicted under the law as an adult. Though there were obvious limitations to his intelligence and intellect, that information was deemed irrelevant and was not taken into consideration for his conviction or his sentencing. His sentence was a length span of life in prison, taking not only his youth but the rest of his life with it, though it was determined that he would be eligible for parole in the year 2048. He was sent to the Columbia Correctional Institution to serve his sentence in Portage, Wisconsin.

Three years later in January of 2010, Brendan Dassey and his attorneys filed a motion that asked for a retrial. This retrial motion was denied almost a full year later by Judge Fox in December. The Wisconsin Court of Appeals stood behind the ruling in January of 2013. The Wisconsin Supreme Court would not even review the case.

Without many other options left, Brendan Dassey's attorneys put together a writ for habeas corpus in December of 2015. This writ asked for Brendan Dassey to either be retried or released on the grounds that his constitutional rights had been violated, because his previous counsel during the trials was ineffective and the only evidence against him (his confession) had been coerced and retracted. In specific, the writ said, "Petitioner Brendan Dassey is in custody pursuant to a state-court judgment of conviction. His conviction, sentence, and confinement are unlawful and were unconstitutionally obtained in violation of his Fifth, Sixth, and Fourteenth Amendment rights. In particular, this federal habeas petition asserts two claims. The first claim asserts that Brendan Dasseyís Sixth Amendment right to the effective assistance of counsel was violated when his pre-trial attorney breached his duty of loyalty by working with the prosecution to secure Brendanís conviction. The second claim asserts that Brendanís Fifth and Fourteenth Amendment rights to due process were violated by the admission of his involuntary confession."

According to the improvements called for within the Juvenile Interrogation Protection Law in Wisconsin, "The United States Supreme Court describes a custodial interrogation as an interrogation where: 'a reasonable person would have felt he or she was not at liberty to terminate the interrogation and leave.' Even if a minor has the legal right to get up and walk out, the vast majority of minors would have no idea that they had that option. Therefore, it is reasonable to view any interrogation of a minor as a custodial interrogation. For these reasons the, Juvenile Interrogation Protection Law in Wisconsin should impose the following safeguards: Require that an attorney be present during any custodial interrogation of a minor. This should be viewed as a nonwaivable right. Require law enforcement to inform a minor before an interrogation begins that he or she could be charged as an adult based on information obtained during an interrogation. Wisconsin law currently falls short, as it only requires law enforcement to immediately attempt to notify the childís parent or guardian."

The federal magistrate by the name of William E. Duffin officially concluded that the confession that was given had been coerced, leading to him overturning the conviction and ordering that Brendan Dassey be released from imprisonment if the state was not going to continue trying to prosecute him through a retrial. The only real evidence that they had that pointed to Brendan Dassey's inclusion in the murder and cover up was his confession. However, William E. Duffin's ruling went through the U.S. Court of Appeals for the Seventh Circuit and was then appealed by the state Justice Department. Their intention was to stop Brendan Dassey from being released, at least until another hearing could be held in regards to his future. It wasn't until June of 2017 that the Seventh Circuit reached its decision to side with William E. Duffin's ruling. This meant that if the state did not decide to appeal this ruling and bring it all the way to the Supreme Court or retry him, that they would have to dismiss the charges and release him.

The Wisconsin Department of Justice banded together again on July 5th to request an en banc re-rehearing. This new hearing was to be reviewed by the entire panel of the

Seventh Circuit. If this review is taken en banc, or decides to side with the ruling made in June, then those in charge of prosecuting Brendan Dassey will find they have but three options left: to retry Brendan Dassey, to appeal to the Supreme Court, or to dismiss the charges against him. Those that are following the trial have made note of the fact that the only real evidence against Brendan Dassey is his coerced confession. The popular opinion is that with that coerced confession being deemed inadmissible, it is very unlikely that there is enough evidence against Brendan Dassey to even pretend to try him against these charges again.

As of February 14th of 2017, Brendan Dassey was still awaiting word on his fate. As a twenty-seven year old adult that had spent the last ten years incarcerated for a crime he is no longer officially charged for and has not been officially tried for, the last word on his case was that it could be months until there is any actual word on his case.

Media Coverage of Steven Avery

Due to the rarity of the full circumstances around Steven Avery's prosecution, the cases against him quickly became known as a sensational piece of news. Because of this, the case was covered by many different media networks on many different platforms. The public radio program Called Radiolab put on a twenty-four minute segment by the title, "Reasonable Doubt," which aired on an episode by the title, "Are You Sure?" On March 26th of 2013, media coverage explored the story of the case through the eyes of Penny Beerntsen, the woman that wrongfully accused him of sexually assaulting her in 1985.

The infamous talk show host and counselor Dr. Phil had two episodes that were centered around Steven Avery and the two trials surrounding the murder of Teresa Halbach. It inspired the creation of several follow up interviews and new written articles with the people that were featured in the documentary; which also included family members and some reporters that had followed the case but had not yet been put in the spotlight so that the public to hear what they had to say.

Taking hold of the sensational court proceedings and the influx of viewers towards real crime television, Netflix released an original documentary series that spanned ten episodes on December 18th of 2015 and called it Making A Murder. The ten episode long series explored the defendants

Steven Avery and Brendan Dassey and their investigations and trials. It also covered the background information and details on the alleged vendetta that the Manitowoc Count police department held against him. In this series, the allegations of police and prosecutorial misconduct were investigated, and allegations of evidence tampering and coercion were also put under scrutiny.

Making A Murderer; And Making A Media Sensation

Many people were surprised by the lack of media coverage during the trials of Steven Avery and his nephew, Brendan Dassey. Netflix capitalized on this fact when it debuted its original documentary series, titled Making A Murderer. This series was released on December 18th of 2015 and featured ten full episodes that covered the criminal charges against Steven Avery and the events that led to his incarceration for the murder of Teresa Halbach. Each episode is between forty-seven and sixty-six minutes long, and it covers the biggest parts of his trials as well as the evidence against him.

It took ten years for the series to finish filming, taking the creators Moira Demos and Laura Ricciardi back and forth between Wisconsin and New York City. The first episode of Making A Murderer was released on Youtube as well as Netflix, which was an unprecedented marketing technique for Netflix before the series aired. No other original program released by Netflix had ever been concurrently aired in that way.

The filmmakers that are responsible for creating this Netflix documentary are two women by the name of Laura Ricciardi and Moira Demon. The two were both graduate students from the film program at Columbia University when they met. Together, they first heard about Steven Avery and his infamous court trial after reading an article in the 2005 New York Times that was focused on his exoneration in the year 2003 and his quick arrest for murder just two years later in 2005. Casual conversation brought them both to admit that they thought Steven Avery would be a good subject for a documentary. Together, they met with executives in charge of programming at both HBO and PBS, but neither of the two networks were interested at all in their project. They did not want to air this potential documentary on their channels. When Netflix originally picked up the series, the contract was for a total of eight episodes. Later, this number was expanded by two, to a total of ten episodes in the first season's series arc.

Looking at the series in the same light as any other television series, it received rave reviews. It has been compared to The Jinx, as seen on HBO, in a favorable light. It has also been favorably compared to the podcast by the name of Serial. Though it has been the center and cause of much controversy, it has been widely viewed in both Manitowoc County and nationwide. It also inspired a petition to be written and passed around in December of 2015, asking the White House to issue official pardons for Steven Avery. This petition was signed more than 500,000 times by different people. However, the White House issued an official statement that reminded the public that the President does not have the authority to pardon a criminal that is under the weight of a state offense.

Regardless, the success of this Netflix original documentary series has been the spark that ignited many different conversations about the criminal justice system and the rules surrounding the way criminals are prosecuted.

The success of the documentary has paid off for its creators, and a second documentary series was announced in July of 2016. It is presumably still being filmed, with the focus being the aftermath of the previous series. It will cover Brendan Dassey's conviction and all of the appeals that have already taken place in accordance to these crimes.

The list of people that are related to the Avery family that appeared on Making A Murderer include:

- Steven Avery: the defendant
- Dolores Avery: Steven Avery's mother
- Allan Avery: Steven Avery's father
- Chuck Avery: Steven Avery's brother

- Brendan Dassey: Steven Avery's nephew; also a defendant
- Bobby Dassey: Brendan Dassey's brother
- Barb Dassey: Brendan Dassey's mother; Steven Avery's sister
- Scott Tadych: married to Barb Dassey
- Kayla Avery: Brendan Dassey's cousin
- Kim Ducat: Steven Avery's cousin
- Carla Chase: Brendan Dassey's cousin; Steven Avery's niece

The defense lawyers that appeared in the documentary series include:

- Dean Stran: Steven Avery's defense
- Jerome Buting: Steven Avery's defense
- Robert Henak: Steven Avery's attorney after conviction

- Stephen Glynn: Steven Avery's civil rights lawyer
- Len Kachinsky: Brendan Dassey's first lawyer
- Mark Fremgen: Brendan Dassey's second lawyer
- Ray Edelstein: Brendan Dassey's second lawyer
- Steven Drizin: Brendan Dassey's attorney after conviction
- Robert Dvorak: Brendan Dassey's attorney after conviction
- Laura Nirider: Brendan Dassey's attorney after conviction

The prosecution lawyers and judges that made appearances in the documentary series include:

- Dennis Vogel: Manitowoc County District Attorney in 1985 for the Beernsten sexual assault
- Ken Kratz: Special prosecutor; Calumet County District Attorney in Halbach murder
- Patrick Willis: Manitowoc County Circuit Court Judge for Steven Avery's trial
- Norm Gahn: Special prosecutor; Milwaukee County Assistant District Attorney
- Jerome Fox: Manitowoc County Circuit Court Judge for Brendan Dassey's trial

The law enforcement officials that were featured on the documentary series include:

- Tom Kocourek: Manitowoc County Sheriff
- Kenneth Petersen: Manitowoc County Sheriff
- Gene Kusche: Manitowoc County Chief Deputy Sheriff
- James Lenk: Lieutenant, Manitowoc County Sheriff's Department
- Andrew Colborn: Sergeant; Manitowoc County Sheriff's Department
- Judy Dvorak: Deputy; Manitowoc County Sheriff's Department
- Tom Fassbender: Investigator; Wisconsin Division of Criminal Investigation
- Mark Wiegert: Sergeant; Calumet County Sheriff's Department

The private investigator featured on the documentary series is a man by the name of Michael O'Kelly and he was hired by Len Kachinsky. The two victims featured in the documentary series are the two women Penny Beerntsen and Teresa Halbach.

Steven Avery's Personal Life After Incarceration

When the charges in the Teresa Halbach case hit Steven Avery, one would think that romance was the last thing on his mind. However, a month after the debut of the Netflix documentary series about him was released, he was engaged to a woman by the name of Lynn Hartman. They had met eight months earlier, sharing conversation through phone calls and letters before finally deciding to meet in person at the correctional facility where he was being held. They kept their relationship a secret, but she claimed that she was still a target for those that wished to talk down to her and threaten her for her relationship with the accused.

According to her, their romance blossomed in a way that was like magic. As a fan of Nancy Grace, Lynn Hartman was assured of Steven Avery's guilt and wanting nothing to do with him. She believed everything that the other woman said about him and was sure that he was guilty. Because of her confidence in her opinion, she refused to watch Making A Murderer. It appeared that the Netflix documentary had been created with the hope of fooling people into thinking that Steven Avery was innocent, despite his guilt. However, Lynn Hartman's daughter kept pestering her and she eventually gave in and gave the series a watch. She eventually started to rethink her stance, deciding that perhaps Steven Avery's guilt wasn't so obvious. From there, she started to change her mind about the man himself.

At the end of the series, Lynn Hartman realized how bad she felt for Steven Avery. She wrote him a letter in support and sent him a handful of photos of herself and let him know that she wanted to support him in any way possible. The woman did not expect to get any kind of reply, but she did. Upon reading his reply, she said that she was given a rare glimpse at the man behind the infamous name Steven Avery. Letters turned into phone calls, and according to her she eventually realized that it wasn't her that was helping him; he was helping her. She claims to have fallen in love with that side of him and the relationship that they developed together. He supported her through a crushing divorce that almost killed her. At the end of their first phone call, Steven Avery said that he was in love with her.

During a phone call in the early hours on September 6th, he proposed to her and the two were engaged.

ìIt was just like magic,î Hartman said about their first meeting. ìThe first moment I laid eyes on him, I just thought he was a teddy bear. The chemistry was there. He came over and sat at the table and we held hands. And it was exactly like I imagined for the months leading up to it. We talked about what we want to do when he gets out. What are the possibilities of our lives together? And do we keep going until it happens? He told me about how much I meant to him, and how much our love meant to him.î And thatís certainly what I needed at the time, after my divorce, and what he needed, too.

She appeared on the Dr. Phil show, giving an interview that put her and her relationship with Steven Avery on television. Steven Avery himself phoned in to be interviewed on the show as well, and he had nothing but good things to say about her. According to him, she spoiled him and made him happy. His happiness with her and the validity of their relationship was seconded by Steven Avery's attorney. She posted photos of the two together on Twitter and captioned it with her words of support.

However, shortly after the Dr. Phil show was recorded, Steven Avery broke off his engagement with Lynn Hartman. According to him, she was nothing more than a gold digger; which was an opinion that many of her critics shared as well. According to her, he still loved her but his family wedged them apart. She has also been quoted as saying that his behavior and advice from Dr. Phil himself are what broke them up. Whatever the truth to the matter is, Steven Avery had his family release statements calling Lynn Hartman a gold digger, saying that she would not answer his phone calls anymore and that she had made thousands of dollars off of his story through booking interviews to talk about their engagement. She continued to take interviews after their engagement ended and she continued to speak positively about him for quite some time. According to her, she still believed him to be innocent. Until she suddenly changed her mind after being called a gold digger and began throwing accusations around that he had threatened her life and the lives of her children. While she had once advocated for his release from incarceration and swore that she thought he was innocent, now that they are no longer together, she has taken it all back by claiming the exact opposite. She says that she fears for her life and hopes that he never gets out of prison.

Since their engagement was broken off, the photos of them together on their first meeting have been poured over and analyzed repeatedly. Many people are of the opinion that Lynn Hartman was obviously uncomfortable and that she appeared to be anything but truly happy to be there. This only backs up the theory that she was only there for the fame and fortune being acquainted with someone as infamous as Steven Avery might bring her.

Another curve ball was thrown when Lynn Hartman took back everything that she had said positively about Steven Avery before and claimed that she had broken up with him. She also claimed that she believed he killed Teresa Halbach, because after she broke up with him, he threatened the lives of herself and her children.

Before Lynn Hartman, there was Sandra Greenman. Sandra and Steven started dating shortly after his trials began in 2005 and continued to share a blissful but platonic relationship long after their engagement was called off. They were engaged for over six full years and according to her, they are still best friends. She only asked him if he had killed Teresa Halbach once, and she took his word when he said he was innocent. An avid supporter of Steven Avery with hopes for him to lead a happy, healthy, and safe life, Sandra Greenman never liked or trusted Lynn Hartman. Her opinion from the very beginning was that Lynn Hartman was nothing more than a gold digger and she had voiced her opinion many times before that relationship sank as well.

She was the one to end her own relationship with him based on the fact that Steven Avery would not convert to Christianity for her, but she still maintains that she thinks he is innocent. Their romantic relationship is long since over, but Sandra still stands in support of Steven Avery. She has been quoted saying that she truly believes he is innocent and that she wants to be there for him, to support him and prove that she does believe he is innocent. According to her, the two of them are still very much in love, but she cannot marry someone that is not Christian. Her husband must share her religious faith. Since their relationship ended, her visits to see him have become fewer and further between, but she claims it has nothing to do with anything negative between the two of them. She still supports him as fully as she did while they were engaged, but it is too painful to see him knowing that she cannot be with him romantically. There is even a photoshopped photo of the two of them in her home, photoshopped to put him in a photo of her that was taken in her backyard. The two have never met outside of the prison he is incarcerated in, because they met after he was arrested and charged, but she wanted to be able to see what it would look like if they were to spend time together outside of the dreary prison; like a normal pair of normal people.

"Steve and I were engaged to be married and I broke it off. It's not that I've ever stopped trying to work for him but it was a religious thing. I cannot marry someone that's not a Christian. Since we broke off the engagement, I've visited him less and less. It's too hard for me. I still love him and want the best for him. I want him out. He calls any time he can and he says I'm being stubborn. But we will see what happens. It's a friendship right now. I don't know how it's going to end and if he gets out, it's a whole different story.: Sandra Greenman is quoted as saying about their engagement and the end of their romantic relationship. "But it doesn't change anything. I will always be behind him and he's my best friend."

Part of her insistence that he convert to Christianity may be attributed to her desire for him to find happiness and absolution. She has been quoted stating that she is concerned for his mental health, and she believes he is harboring an unhealthy amount of resentment inside of him for the people that made it possible for him to have spent so much of his life behind bars for crimes he proclaims he is innocent of. She believes that he needs something to believe in, something to help him get through these hard years and something to help him get passed all of the hurt that has been caused to him; if he is indeed innocently incarcerated and serving time for a crime he did not commit.

The third of Steven Avery's prison relationships was between him and a woman by the name of Jodi Stachowski. Jodi was the first of his prison relationships, with the two of them being together at the time that Making A Murderer was being filmed. She had nothing but good things to say about him when the documentary crew came to speak with her and ask her questions about him, but later recanted everything that she had said, claiming that she had been forced to lie by Steven Avery himself. During the investigation, she was questioned multiple times and never changed her statement, which was that she believed Steven Avery to be innocent. She even spoke about two phone calls that they shared on the night of the murder. Jodi Stachowski herself was incarcerated on a drunk driving charge on the night of the murder, but she did not note anything strange about their calls that night.

She thought it was rather unlikely that he would take a break from raping, killing, and burning Teresa Halbach just to make a few phone calls to her. She also thought it was rather unlikely that he would act normally while on these phone calls, leaving her none-the-wiser to any illicit activities he may have been committing.

After the documentary aired, Jodi returned to television so that she could be interviewed on Nancy Grace. In this interview, she claimed that Steven Avery was not an innocent man. According to her new interview testimony, he was such a bad man that she ate two full boxes of rat poison just so that she could be sent to the hospital and taken away from him. Her previous opinions were all turned on their head, and she claimed that she believed he was guilty.

When asked why, she explained that he had threatened to kill her, her family, and one of her friends.

Still, even Jodi Stachowski admits that whenever she asked Steven Avery about the murder of Teresa Halbach, he would deny having anything to do with it. Her decision to come forward and change her public opinion was not made based on evidence or any confession made to her, instead, it was made solely on a desire to "tell the truth." She wanted her story to be told.

Her story includes an abusive two year relationship, with hospital reports that were presented to the audience during the show that hosted her interview that back up her claims. After eating two boxes of rat poison so that she would be sent to the hospital and away from him, she asked the staff there to get the police to help her and told them her story.

Other highlights of this interview with Jodi Stachowski include her opinions on Teresa Halbach's death and the possible involvement of Brendan Dassey. She believes that the young nephew of Steven Avery is innocent, despite her theory that Steven Avery is not. She also claims that she was supposed to testify against her ex, but nobody ever called on her when the time came. She maintains that he is still sending her threatening messages from his place in prison, and she states that she has given these threatening messages to the police.

Jodi also claims that because she was forced to lie to the creators of the Netflix documentary series, she had asked them not to include her in their final edit. When she was asked to take part in one final interview to wrap the series up right before it aired, she declined. According to her, the documentary is nothing but lies, though she has admitted that she hasn't even watched it.

According to Sandra Greenman, who is seventy-three to Steven Avery's fifty-five, there are very few people that take the time to visit Steven in prison. His visitor limit is twelve while he's locked up in prison, but Sandra Greenman has stated that there are far fewer people that actually come to see him. Usually, the only people that go to visit him are his parents and Sandra Greenman. There is a maximum number of people that he is allowed to have placed on his visitor's list, but he has not ever gotten close to filling those spots. He does have permission to make phone calls as well, but even those are generally reserved for his parents and Sandra Greenman. Even with permission to make calls, he still only makes just a few of them a week.

His brothers, Charles and Early, have both been noted as absent. Neither have gone to visit him even once in the whole nine year span of time that he has spent behind bars for the murder of Teresa Halbach. It may have been a combination of anger and frustration, but Steven Avery once proposed that the two of them may have been the cause of Teresa Halbach's murder, which would explain their decision to stay as far away from the man that was serving time for her murder as possible. It was in court paperwork that was filled out and filed by

Steven Avery himself in 2009 that the speculated allegations were made. These speculations were made right after he was given the sentence of life without parole, so it is possible that they were made out of simple frustration. TMZ still managed to obtain these court papers and shared them with the public. The Avery brother's mother, Dolores Avery, has been questioned in regards to Steven Avery's 2009 speculations as well. When she was asked about the idea that her other two sons might have been involved instead of Steven and Brendan, she was quick to defend all three of her sons. According to her, they were all innocent and while she did not hold it against him, these allegations were likely made in desperation after Steven Avery realized that he had managed to get free of a wrongful conviction after spending eighteen years behind bars only to be sent back to die in prison only two years after finally earning his freedom in 2003. She speculated that he felt he had to do something and just did not know what to do. She firmly believes that the allegations have nothing to do with Steven Avery's brothers and have more to do with the situation and the volatile state of the imprisoned man's emotions.

In an interview, Dolores Avery was quoted as saying, "It's a shame, it split the family apart,' Sandy said. 'A lot of it was [because of] the Dassey confession which the prosecution used against Steve. There was a lot of bad blood there for a long time. I'm not involved but I think things are much better now,' she said. 'I think the relationship between Barbara and her parents seems terrific now. They realized that it wasn't Brendan talking and he was just trying to say something to satisfy the interrogators."

Despite the lack of physical interaction with his family. Steven Avery does have a massive fan following, and he does get letters and phone calls from people that want to show him their support. Sandra Greenman has consistently made sure that his messages can reach the outside world as well, and she's been seen making various posts on her social media accounts over the years on Steven Avery's behalf. According to her, he really enjoys the letters that he gets and wants to express his gratitude to his supporters. Sandra Greenman is also credited with having begged Kathleen Zellner to take on Steven Avery's case. As one of the biggest, high profile attorneys in

Chicago, she came onto the case with a long list of victories taken on post-conviction cases already hanging off of her belt.

Just two years ago, Steven Avery was moved from the correctional facility that he had served most of his time at and brought to Boscobel to continue serving his sentence in a maximum-security prison. This prison is a total of four hours away from Manitowoc County, so his family has to drive four hours to see him. Waupun Correctional Institute is only ninety miles away from it, however.

Though his brothers have not seen him since he was arrested for the murder of Teresa Halbach, his cousin by the name of Kim Ducat has seen him once. They get along well, despite not seeing each other beyond the once. While he was a resident at the

Boscobel prison, he got a few visits from his daughter, Jenny. She is the only one of his kids to have gone to see him and she did not go to see him more than those few times. They didn't get to grow up with him in their lives so they don't really know him. His sister Barbara visited once as well, but her visit was made in order to bring their parents to see him. It is possible that she would not have gone if they had been able to get a ride with someone else and she has not gone to see him since.

Many people still believe that Steven Avery is guilty, while others are convinced of his innocence beyond reasonable doubt. The Netflix series sparked new interest in the case and has brought about new theories and new inquiries. It is undeniably suspicious that Steven Avery was in the middle of a $36 million civil lawsuit against Manitowoc County when he was arrested and charged with a new crime; a crime that would put him behind bars for life. But conversely, the fact that he was arrested, charged, and convicted of such a heinous crime after being found innocent of the previous charge of sexual assault puts weight behind the idea that he wasn't as innocent as he seemed. Whether it was the simple, angry vendetta of a police force whose officer was married to someone that Steven Avery upset or the simple consequences of his unlawful actions and abusive nature finally catching up with him may never be revealed for certain. However, the fate of the man himself should be concluded soon and the legal ordeals that have spanned almost the full length of his life may be over soon.

Printed in Great Britain
by Amazon